50 Gluten-Free Delights Recipes

By: Kelly Johnson

Table of Contents

- Almond Flour Pancakes
- Quinoa Salad with Avocado
- Gluten-Free Chocolate Chip Cookies
- Cauliflower Crust Pizza
- Coconut Flour Brownies
- Grilled Chicken with Lemon Herb Dressing
- Zucchini Noodles with Pesto
- Rice Paper Spring Rolls
- Gluten-Free Banana Bread
- Quinoa and Black Bean Stuffed Peppers
- Baked Sweet Potato Fries
- Gluten-Free Vegan Cupcakes
- Chia Pudding with Berries
- Eggplant Parmesan
- Gluten-Free Oatmeal Cookies
- Sweet Potato and Black Bean Tacos
- Avocado and Chickpea Salad
- Gluten-Free Blueberry Muffins
- Grilled Shrimp Skewers
- Almond Butter Energy Bites
- Baked Chicken with Herbs
- Gluten-Free Waffles
- Roasted Brussels Sprouts with Balsamic
- Flourless Chocolate Cake
- Cucumber and Tomato Salad
- Grilled Portobello Mushrooms
- Spaghetti Squash Primavera
- Gluten-Free Veggie Burger
- Lemon Garlic Roasted Chicken
- Stuffed Acorn Squash
- Sweet Potato Hash
- Gluten-Free Apple Crisp
- Roasted Cauliflower with Turmeric
- Paleo Granola
- Coconut Curry Shrimp

- Gluten-Free Rice Pudding
- Avocado Toast on Gluten-Free Bread
- Chickpea and Spinach Stew
- Gluten-Free Pizza with Toppings
- Pecan-Crusted Salmon
- Spicy Roasted Chickpeas
- Flourless Almond Cake
- Grilled Veggie Kebabs
- Gluten-Free Frittata
- Roasted Red Pepper Soup
- Gluten-Free Chocolate Mousse
- Quinoa and Vegetable Stir-Fry
- Baked Falafel
- Gluten-Free Carrot Cake
- Coconut Macaroons

Almond Flour Pancakes

Ingredients:

- 1 cup almond flour
- 2 large eggs
- 1/4 cup unsweetened almond milk (or any milk of choice)
- 1 tablespoon coconut oil or butter, melted
- 1 teaspoon vanilla extract
- 1 teaspoon baking powder
- 1/4 teaspoon salt
- Sweetener to taste (e.g., maple syrup, stevia, or honey)
- Butter or oil for cooking

Instructions:

1. In a bowl, whisk together the almond flour, baking powder, salt, and any sweetener you choose.
2. In another bowl, beat the eggs and add the almond milk, melted coconut oil (or butter), and vanilla extract.
3. Combine the wet and dry ingredients, stirring until well-mixed and smooth.
4. Heat a non-stick pan or griddle over medium heat and lightly grease with butter or oil.
5. Pour a small amount of the batter onto the pan to form pancakes of your desired size. Cook for 2-3 minutes on one side, until bubbles form on the surface, then flip and cook for another 1-2 minutes until golden brown.
6. Serve warm with toppings like maple syrup, fresh fruit, or nuts.

Quinoa Salad with Avocado

Ingredients:

- 1 cup quinoa
- 2 cups water or vegetable broth
- 1 ripe avocado, diced
- 1/2 cup cherry tomatoes, halved
- 1/4 cup red onion, finely diced
- 1/4 cup fresh cilantro, chopped
- 2 tablespoons olive oil
- 1 tablespoon lime juice
- Salt and pepper to taste

Instructions:

1. Rinse the quinoa under cold water and place it in a saucepan with the water or vegetable broth. Bring to a boil, then reduce heat and simmer for 15 minutes, or until the quinoa is cooked and the liquid is absorbed. Let it cool.
2. In a large bowl, combine the cooled quinoa, diced avocado, cherry tomatoes, red onion, and cilantro.
3. Drizzle with olive oil and lime juice, then toss to combine.
4. Season with salt and pepper to taste. Serve chilled or at room temperature.

Gluten-Free Chocolate Chip Cookies
Ingredients:

- 1 1/4 cups gluten-free all-purpose flour
- 1/2 teaspoon baking soda
- 1/4 teaspoon salt
- 1/2 cup butter, softened
- 1/2 cup brown sugar
- 1/4 cup granulated sugar
- 1 teaspoon vanilla extract
- 1 large egg
- 1 cup gluten-free chocolate chips

Instructions:

1. Preheat the oven to 350°F (175°C) and line a baking sheet with parchment paper.
2. In a medium bowl, whisk together the gluten-free flour, baking soda, and salt.
3. In a separate large bowl, cream together the butter, brown sugar, and granulated sugar until smooth and fluffy.
4. Add the egg and vanilla extract to the butter mixture and mix well.
5. Gradually add the dry ingredients to the wet ingredients, stirring until combined.
6. Fold in the chocolate chips.
7. Scoop tablespoon-sized portions of dough onto the prepared baking sheet, spacing them about 2 inches apart.
8. Bake for 10-12 minutes, or until the edges are golden. Allow to cool on a wire rack.

Cauliflower Crust Pizza
Ingredients:

- 1 medium head of cauliflower
- 1/2 cup shredded mozzarella cheese
- 1/4 cup grated Parmesan cheese
- 1 large egg
- 1 teaspoon dried oregano
- 1/2 teaspoon garlic powder
- Salt and pepper to taste
- Your favorite pizza toppings (e.g., marinara sauce, mozzarella cheese, veggies, pepperoni, etc.)

Instructions:

1. Preheat the oven to 400°F (200°C) and line a baking sheet with parchment paper.
2. Cut the cauliflower into florets and pulse them in a food processor until they resemble rice-sized pieces.
3. Microwave the cauliflower for 5-6 minutes until softened, then place it in a clean kitchen towel and squeeze out excess moisture.
4. In a bowl, mix the cauliflower, mozzarella cheese, Parmesan cheese, egg, oregano, garlic powder, salt, and pepper.
5. Spread the mixture onto the prepared baking sheet, shaping it into a round crust.
6. Bake for 15-20 minutes, or until the crust is golden and crispy.
7. Remove from the oven and add your desired pizza toppings.
8. Bake for an additional 5-10 minutes, or until the cheese is melted and bubbly.
9. Slice and serve warm.

Coconut Flour Brownies
Ingredients:

- 1/2 cup coconut flour
- 1/4 cup unsweetened cocoa powder
- 1/2 teaspoon baking soda
- 1/4 teaspoon salt
- 1/4 cup melted coconut oil
- 1/4 cup maple syrup
- 2 large eggs
- 1 teaspoon vanilla extract
- 1/4 cup unsweetened almond milk
- 1/4 cup chocolate chips (optional)

Instructions:

1. Preheat the oven to 350°F (175°C) and grease or line a baking pan.
2. In a medium bowl, whisk together the coconut flour, cocoa powder, baking soda, and salt.
3. In another bowl, mix the melted coconut oil, maple syrup, eggs, and vanilla extract.
4. Add the wet ingredients to the dry ingredients and stir to combine.
5. Gradually add the almond milk to achieve a thick batter. Fold in chocolate chips if using.
6. Pour the batter into the prepared baking pan and smooth the top.
7. Bake for 20-25 minutes or until a toothpick inserted comes out clean.
8. Let the brownies cool before cutting into squares.

Grilled Chicken with Lemon Herb Dressing

Ingredients:

- 4 boneless, skinless chicken breasts
- 2 tablespoons olive oil
- 1 tablespoon lemon juice
- 1 tablespoon fresh parsley, chopped
- 1 teaspoon garlic powder
- Salt and pepper to taste

Instructions:

1. Preheat the grill to medium-high heat.
2. In a small bowl, whisk together the olive oil, lemon juice, parsley, garlic powder, salt, and pepper.
3. Brush the chicken breasts with the lemon herb dressing.
4. Grill the chicken for 5-7 minutes on each side, or until fully cooked and no longer pink in the center.
5. Serve with extra lemon wedges and herbs if desired.

Zucchini Noodles with Pesto

Ingredients:

- 2 large zucchinis, spiralized into noodles
- 1/2 cup pesto (store-bought or homemade)
- 1 tablespoon olive oil
- Salt and pepper to taste
- Parmesan cheese (optional)

Instructions:

1. Heat olive oil in a skillet over medium heat.
2. Add the zucchini noodles and sauté for 2-3 minutes until just tender.
3. Stir in the pesto and toss to coat the noodles evenly.
4. Season with salt and pepper to taste.
5. Serve with a sprinkle of Parmesan cheese, if desired.

Rice Paper Spring Rolls
Ingredients:

- 8 rice paper wrappers
- 1 cup shredded lettuce
- 1/2 cup julienned carrots
- 1/2 cup cucumber, julienned
- 1/4 cup fresh cilantro
- 1/4 cup fresh mint leaves
- 1/2 cup cooked shrimp or chicken (optional)
- Peanut or hoisin dipping sauce

Instructions:

1. Dip one rice paper wrapper into warm water for 10-15 seconds until softened.
2. Lay the wrapper on a flat surface and layer a small amount of lettuce, carrots, cucumber, cilantro, mint, and shrimp or chicken in the center.
3. Roll up the rice paper, folding in the edges as you go.
4. Repeat with the remaining wrappers and ingredients.
5. Serve the spring rolls with peanut or hoisin dipping sauce.

Gluten-Free Banana Bread

Ingredients:

- 2 ripe bananas, mashed
- 2 large eggs
- 1/4 cup melted coconut oil
- 1/4 cup maple syrup
- 1 1/2 cups gluten-free all-purpose flour
- 1 teaspoon baking soda
- 1/2 teaspoon salt
- 1/2 teaspoon cinnamon
- 1/2 teaspoon vanilla extract

Instructions:

1. Preheat the oven to 350°F (175°C) and grease a loaf pan.
2. In a bowl, combine the mashed bananas, eggs, coconut oil, maple syrup, and vanilla extract.
3. In another bowl, whisk together the gluten-free flour, baking soda, salt, and cinnamon.
4. Gradually add the dry ingredients to the wet ingredients and stir until combined.
5. Pour the batter into the prepared loaf pan and bake for 50-60 minutes or until a toothpick comes out clean.
6. Let the banana bread cool before slicing.

Quinoa and Black Bean Stuffed Peppers
Ingredients:

- 4 large bell peppers, tops cut off and seeds removed
- 1 cup cooked quinoa
- 1 can (15 oz) black beans, drained and rinsed
- 1/2 cup corn kernels (fresh or frozen)
- 1/2 teaspoon cumin
- 1/2 teaspoon chili powder
- 1/4 cup shredded cheese (optional)
- Salt and pepper to taste

Instructions:

1. Preheat the oven to 375°F (190°C).
2. In a bowl, combine the cooked quinoa, black beans, corn, cumin, chili powder, salt, and pepper.
3. Stuff the bell peppers with the quinoa mixture.
4. Place the stuffed peppers in a baking dish and cover with foil.
5. Bake for 25-30 minutes, then remove the foil and sprinkle with cheese if desired.
6. Bake for an additional 5 minutes until the cheese melts.

Baked Sweet Potato Fries
Ingredients:

- 2 large sweet potatoes, peeled and cut into fries
- 2 tablespoons olive oil
- 1 teaspoon paprika
- 1/2 teaspoon garlic powder
- Salt and pepper to taste

Instructions:

1. Preheat the oven to 425°F (220°C) and line a baking sheet with parchment paper.
2. Toss the sweet potato fries in olive oil, paprika, garlic powder, salt, and pepper.
3. Spread the fries in a single layer on the baking sheet.
4. Bake for 25-30 minutes, flipping halfway through, until crispy and golden.

Gluten-Free Vegan Cupcakes
Ingredients:

- 1 1/2 cups gluten-free all-purpose flour
- 1/2 teaspoon baking soda
- 1/2 teaspoon baking powder
- 1/4 teaspoon salt
- 1/2 cup almond milk
- 1/4 cup maple syrup
- 1/4 cup coconut oil, melted
- 1 teaspoon vanilla extract

Instructions:

1. Preheat the oven to 350°F (175°C) and line a muffin tin with cupcake liners.
2. In a bowl, whisk together the dry ingredients (flour, baking soda, baking powder, and salt).
3. In another bowl, combine the wet ingredients (almond milk, maple syrup, coconut oil, and vanilla extract).
4. Stir the wet ingredients into the dry ingredients until combined.
5. Divide the batter evenly among the cupcake liners.
6. Bake for 18-20 minutes, or until a toothpick comes out clean.

Chia Pudding with Berries
Ingredients:

- 1/2 cup chia seeds
- 2 cups almond milk
- 1 tablespoon maple syrup
- 1/2 teaspoon vanilla extract
- 1/2 cup mixed berries

Instructions:

1. In a bowl, combine the chia seeds, almond milk, maple syrup, and vanilla extract.
2. Stir well and refrigerate for at least 2 hours or overnight.
3. Once the chia pudding has thickened, top with fresh berries before serving.

Eggplant Parmesan
Ingredients:

- 2 medium eggplants, sliced into rounds
- 1 cup gluten-free breadcrumbs
- 1/2 cup grated Parmesan cheese
- 1 cup marinara sauce
- 1 1/2 cups shredded mozzarella cheese
- 1 tablespoon olive oil
- Salt and pepper to taste

Instructions:

1. Preheat the oven to 375°F (190°C).
2. Season the eggplant slices with salt and pepper, then dip them into breadcrumbs.
3. Heat olive oil in a skillet and cook the eggplant slices for 2-3 minutes on each side, until golden.
4. In a baking dish, layer the eggplant slices, marinara sauce, and mozzarella cheese.
5. Repeat the layers, then top with Parmesan cheese.
6. Bake for 25-30 minutes until the cheese is bubbly and golden.

Gluten-Free Oatmeal Cookies
Ingredients:

- 1 cup gluten-free rolled oats
- 1/2 cup almond flour
- 1/4 teaspoon baking soda
- 1/4 teaspoon cinnamon
- 1/4 teaspoon salt
- 1/4 cup coconut oil, melted
- 1/4 cup honey or maple syrup
- 1 egg
- 1 teaspoon vanilla extract
- 1/4 cup raisins or chocolate chips (optional)

Instructions:

1. Preheat the oven to 350°F (175°C) and line a baking sheet with parchment paper.
2. In a bowl, combine the oats, almond flour, baking soda, cinnamon, and salt.
3. In a separate bowl, mix together the melted coconut oil, honey or maple syrup, egg, and vanilla extract.
4. Add the wet ingredients to the dry ingredients and stir until combined.
5. Fold in raisins or chocolate chips if using.
6. Drop spoonfuls of dough onto the baking sheet and flatten slightly.
7. Bake for 10-12 minutes, or until golden brown.
8. Let the cookies cool on the baking sheet before transferring to a wire rack.

Sweet Potato and Black Bean Tacos
Ingredients:

- 2 medium sweet potatoes, peeled and diced
- 1 tablespoon olive oil
- 1 teaspoon chili powder
- 1/2 teaspoon cumin
- Salt and pepper to taste
- 1 can (15 oz) black beans, drained and rinsed
- 8 small corn tortillas
- 1 avocado, sliced
- Fresh cilantro, for garnish
- Lime wedges, for serving

Instructions:

1. Preheat the oven to 400°F (200°C).
2. Toss the diced sweet potatoes in olive oil, chili powder, cumin, salt, and pepper.
3. Spread the sweet potatoes in a single layer on a baking sheet and roast for 25-30 minutes, or until tender.
4. Warm the tortillas in a skillet or microwave.
5. To assemble, divide the roasted sweet potatoes and black beans among the tortillas.
6. Top with sliced avocado, cilantro, and a squeeze of lime juice.

Avocado and Chickpea Salad

Ingredients:

- 1 can (15 oz) chickpeas, drained and rinsed
- 1 avocado, diced
- 1/4 red onion, thinly sliced
- 1/4 cup chopped cucumber
- 1 tablespoon olive oil
- 1 tablespoon lemon juice
- Salt and pepper to taste
- Fresh parsley, for garnish

Instructions:

1. In a large bowl, combine the chickpeas, avocado, red onion, and cucumber.
2. Drizzle with olive oil and lemon juice, then toss to combine.
3. Season with salt and pepper to taste.
4. Garnish with fresh parsley and serve immediately.

Gluten-Free Blueberry Muffins
Ingredients:

- 1 1/2 cups gluten-free all-purpose flour
- 1/2 teaspoon baking powder
- 1/4 teaspoon baking soda
- 1/4 teaspoon salt
- 1/4 cup coconut sugar or honey
- 1/2 cup almond milk
- 1/4 cup melted coconut oil
- 1 teaspoon vanilla extract
- 1 large egg
- 1 cup fresh or frozen blueberries

Instructions:

1. Preheat the oven to 350°F (175°C) and line a muffin tin with paper liners.
2. In a bowl, whisk together the gluten-free flour, baking powder, baking soda, salt, and coconut sugar.
3. In another bowl, combine the almond milk, coconut oil, vanilla extract, and egg.
4. Add the wet ingredients to the dry ingredients and mix until just combined.
5. Gently fold in the blueberries.
6. Divide the batter evenly among the muffin cups.
7. Bake for 18-20 minutes, or until a toothpick inserted comes out clean.

Grilled Shrimp Skewers
Ingredients:

- 1 lb large shrimp, peeled and deveined
- 2 tablespoons olive oil
- 1 tablespoon lemon juice
- 2 garlic cloves, minced
- 1 teaspoon smoked paprika
- Salt and pepper to taste
- Fresh parsley, for garnish

Instructions:

1. Preheat the grill to medium-high heat.
2. In a bowl, combine the olive oil, lemon juice, garlic, smoked paprika, salt, and pepper.
3. Toss the shrimp in the marinade and let sit for 10-15 minutes.
4. Thread the shrimp onto skewers.
5. Grill the shrimp for 2-3 minutes per side, or until pink and cooked through.
6. Garnish with fresh parsley and serve.

Almond Butter Energy Bites
Ingredients:

- 1/2 cup almond butter
- 1/2 cup rolled oats (gluten-free if needed)
- 1/4 cup honey or maple syrup
- 1/4 cup mini chocolate chips (optional)
- 1/4 teaspoon vanilla extract
- Pinch of salt

Instructions:

1. In a bowl, combine all ingredients and mix until fully combined.
2. Roll the mixture into small bite-sized balls.
3. Place the energy bites on a baking sheet lined with parchment paper.
4. Chill in the refrigerator for 30 minutes before serving.

Baked Chicken with Herbs
Ingredients:

- 4 bone-in chicken thighs
- 2 tablespoons olive oil
- 1 tablespoon fresh rosemary, chopped
- 1 tablespoon fresh thyme, chopped
- 2 garlic cloves, minced
- Salt and pepper to taste

Instructions:

1. Preheat the oven to 400°F (200°C).
2. In a small bowl, combine the olive oil, rosemary, thyme, garlic, salt, and pepper.
3. Rub the mixture over the chicken thighs.
4. Place the chicken on a baking sheet and bake for 35-40 minutes, or until the chicken reaches an internal temperature of 165°F (75°C).
5. Let rest for 5 minutes before serving.

Gluten-Free Waffles
Ingredients:

- 1 1/2 cups gluten-free all-purpose flour
- 1 tablespoon sugar
- 1 teaspoon baking powder
- 1/2 teaspoon baking soda
- 1/4 teaspoon salt
- 1 cup almond milk
- 1 large egg
- 1/4 cup melted coconut oil
- 1 teaspoon vanilla extract

Instructions:

1. Preheat your waffle iron according to the manufacturer's instructions.
2. In a bowl, whisk together the flour, sugar, baking powder, baking soda, and salt.
3. In another bowl, whisk together the almond milk, egg, melted coconut oil, and vanilla extract.
4. Add the wet ingredients to the dry ingredients and mix until smooth.
5. Pour the batter onto the preheated waffle iron and cook according to the manufacturer's instructions.
6. Serve with your favorite toppings.

Roasted Brussels Sprouts with Balsamic

Ingredients:

- 1 lb Brussels sprouts, trimmed and halved
- 2 tablespoons olive oil
- 1 tablespoon balsamic vinegar
- Salt and pepper to taste
- 1/4 cup toasted almonds, chopped (optional)

Instructions:

1. Preheat the oven to 400°F (200°C).
2. Toss the Brussels sprouts with olive oil, balsamic vinegar, salt, and pepper.
3. Spread them in a single layer on a baking sheet.
4. Roast for 20-25 minutes, or until golden and crispy on the edges.
5. Garnish with toasted almonds if desired.

Flourless Chocolate Cake

Ingredients:

- 1/2 cup unsalted butter
- 8 oz dark chocolate, chopped
- 3/4 cup sugar
- 3 large eggs
- 1 teaspoon vanilla extract
- Pinch of salt

Instructions:

1. Preheat the oven to 350°F (175°C) and grease a round cake pan.
2. Melt the butter and dark chocolate together in a heatproof bowl over a double boiler or in the microwave, stirring occasionally.
3. Once melted, remove from heat and stir in the sugar, eggs, vanilla extract, and salt.
4. Pour the batter into the prepared cake pan and smooth the top.
5. Bake for 20-25 minutes, or until a toothpick inserted comes out with a few moist crumbs.
6. Let the cake cool before removing it from the pan and serving.

Cucumber and Tomato Salad
Ingredients:

- 2 cups cherry tomatoes, halved
- 1 cucumber, thinly sliced
- 1/4 red onion, thinly sliced
- 1 tablespoon olive oil
- 1 tablespoon red wine vinegar
- 1 teaspoon honey or maple syrup
- Salt and pepper to taste
- Fresh basil, for garnish

Instructions:

1. In a bowl, combine the tomatoes, cucumber, and red onion.
2. In a small bowl, whisk together the olive oil, red wine vinegar, honey, salt, and pepper.
3. Pour the dressing over the vegetables and toss to combine.
4. Garnish with fresh basil and serve immediately.

Grilled Portobello Mushrooms
Ingredients:

- 4 large Portobello mushrooms, cleaned and stems removed
- 2 tablespoons olive oil
- 1 tablespoon balsamic vinegar
- 2 garlic cloves, minced
- 1 teaspoon dried oregano
- Salt and pepper to taste

Instructions:

1. Preheat the grill to medium-high heat.
2. In a bowl, combine the olive oil, balsamic vinegar, garlic, oregano, salt, and pepper.
3. Brush the mushroom caps with the marinade and let them sit for 10-15 minutes.
4. Grill the mushrooms for 5-7 minutes per side, or until tender.
5. Serve as a main dish or alongside other grilled vegetables.

Spaghetti Squash Primavera
Ingredients:

- 1 medium spaghetti squash
- 1 tablespoon olive oil
- 1 zucchini, sliced
- 1 bell pepper, diced
- 1/2 cup cherry tomatoes, halved
- 2 garlic cloves, minced
- Salt and pepper to taste
- Fresh basil, for garnish
- Grated Parmesan (optional)

Instructions:

1. Preheat the oven to 400°F (200°C).
2. Cut the spaghetti squash in half lengthwise and remove the seeds.
3. Drizzle with olive oil, season with salt and pepper, and place the squash cut side down on a baking sheet.
4. Roast for 30-40 minutes, or until the squash is tender and strands can be scraped with a fork.
5. While the squash roasts, heat olive oil in a pan and sauté zucchini, bell pepper, and tomatoes until softened.
6. Add garlic and cook for an additional 1-2 minutes.
7. Scrape the spaghetti squash strands into a bowl, mix with the sautéed vegetables, and garnish with fresh basil and grated Parmesan.

Gluten-Free Veggie Burger
Ingredients:

- 1 can (15 oz) black beans, drained and mashed
- 1 cup cooked quinoa
- 1/2 cup grated carrot
- 1/4 cup finely chopped onion
- 1/4 cup breadcrumbs (gluten-free)
- 1 tablespoon ground flaxseed
- 1 tablespoon soy sauce or tamari
- 1 teaspoon garlic powder
- Salt and pepper to taste

Instructions:

1. In a large bowl, combine the mashed black beans, cooked quinoa, grated carrot, chopped onion, breadcrumbs, ground flaxseed, soy sauce, garlic powder, salt, and pepper.
2. Mix until fully combined and form into patties.
3. Heat a skillet over medium heat and lightly oil it.
4. Cook the patties for 4-5 minutes on each side, or until golden brown and heated through.
5. Serve with your favorite toppings and a gluten-free bun.

Lemon Garlic Roasted Chicken
Ingredients:

- 4 bone-in chicken thighs
- 2 tablespoons olive oil
- 2 garlic cloves, minced
- 1 lemon, sliced
- 1 teaspoon dried thyme
- Salt and pepper to taste

Instructions:

1. Preheat the oven to 400°F (200°C).
2. In a bowl, mix the olive oil, minced garlic, lemon juice, thyme, salt, and pepper.
3. Rub the mixture over the chicken thighs and place the lemon slices on top.
4. Roast the chicken for 35-40 minutes, or until the internal temperature reaches 165°F (75°C).
5. Serve with roasted vegetables or a side salad.

Stuffed Acorn Squash
Ingredients:

- 2 acorn squash, halved and seeds removed
- 1 tablespoon olive oil
- 1/2 cup cooked quinoa
- 1/4 cup dried cranberries
- 1/4 cup chopped pecans
- 1 teaspoon cinnamon
- Salt and pepper to taste

Instructions:

1. Preheat the oven to 375°F (190°C).
2. Drizzle the squash halves with olive oil, season with salt and pepper, and place them cut side down on a baking sheet.
3. Roast for 25-30 minutes, or until the flesh is tender.
4. In a bowl, combine the cooked quinoa, dried cranberries, chopped pecans, cinnamon, salt, and pepper.
5. Once the squash is roasted, stuff it with the quinoa mixture and return to the oven for an additional 5-10 minutes.

Sweet Potato Hash
Ingredients:

- 2 medium sweet potatoes, peeled and diced
- 1 tablespoon olive oil
- 1 red bell pepper, diced
- 1 onion, diced
- 2 garlic cloves, minced
- 1 teaspoon paprika
- Salt and pepper to taste

Instructions:

1. Heat olive oil in a large skillet over medium heat.
2. Add the diced sweet potatoes and cook for 10-12 minutes, or until they start to soften.
3. Add the bell pepper, onion, garlic, paprika, salt, and pepper, and cook for an additional 5-7 minutes.
4. Serve as a breakfast or side dish.

Gluten-Free Apple Crisp
Ingredients:

- 4 cups apples, peeled and sliced
- 1 tablespoon lemon juice
- 1 tablespoon maple syrup
- 1 teaspoon cinnamon
- 1/2 cup gluten-free oats
- 1/4 cup almond flour
- 2 tablespoons coconut oil, melted
- 1/4 cup chopped walnuts (optional)

Instructions:

1. Preheat the oven to 350°F (175°C).
2. In a bowl, toss the sliced apples with lemon juice, maple syrup, and cinnamon.
3. Spread the apples in a baking dish.
4. In a separate bowl, combine the oats, almond flour, melted coconut oil, and chopped walnuts.
5. Sprinkle the oat mixture over the apples.
6. Bake for 30-35 minutes, or until the apples are tender and the topping is golden brown.

Roasted Cauliflower with Turmeric

Ingredients:

- 1 head cauliflower, cut into florets
- 2 tablespoons olive oil
- 1 teaspoon turmeric
- 1/2 teaspoon cumin
- Salt and pepper to taste

Instructions:

1. Preheat the oven to 400°F (200°C).
2. Toss the cauliflower florets with olive oil, turmeric, cumin, salt, and pepper.
3. Spread the cauliflower on a baking sheet in a single layer.
4. Roast for 20-25 minutes, or until golden and tender.

Paleo Granola
Ingredients:

- 2 cups mixed nuts (almonds, cashews, walnuts), chopped
- 1 cup unsweetened shredded coconut
- 1/4 cup chia seeds
- 1/4 cup honey or maple syrup
- 1 tablespoon coconut oil, melted
- 1 teaspoon cinnamon
- 1/4 teaspoon salt

Instructions:

1. Preheat the oven to 325°F (165°C).
2. In a bowl, mix together the nuts, coconut, chia seeds, cinnamon, and salt.
3. In a separate bowl, combine the honey or maple syrup and melted coconut oil.
4. Pour the wet ingredients over the dry ingredients and stir to combine.
5. Spread the mixture onto a baking sheet in a single layer.
6. Bake for 15-20 minutes, stirring halfway through. Let it cool completely before storing.

Coconut Curry Shrimp
Ingredients:

- 1 lb shrimp, peeled and deveined
- 1 tablespoon olive oil
- 1 can (14 oz) coconut milk
- 1 tablespoon red curry paste
- 1 teaspoon ginger, grated
- 2 garlic cloves, minced
- 1 tablespoon lime juice
- Fresh cilantro, for garnish

Instructions:

1. Heat olive oil in a large pan over medium heat.
2. Add the shrimp and cook for 2-3 minutes per side, until pink and cooked through.
3. Remove the shrimp from the pan and set aside.
4. In the same pan, add the coconut milk, curry paste, ginger, and garlic.
5. Simmer for 5-7 minutes, then add the cooked shrimp back into the pan.
6. Stir in the lime juice and garnish with fresh cilantro before serving.

Gluten-Free Rice Pudding
Ingredients:

- 1 cup short-grain rice
- 4 cups coconut milk (or any non-dairy milk)
- 1/4 cup maple syrup
- 1 teaspoon vanilla extract
- 1/2 teaspoon ground cinnamon
- 1/4 teaspoon salt
- 1/2 cup raisins (optional)

Instructions:

1. In a medium saucepan, combine the rice, coconut milk, maple syrup, vanilla extract, cinnamon, and salt.
2. Bring to a boil over medium-high heat.
3. Once boiling, reduce the heat to low and simmer, covered, for 30-35 minutes, or until the rice is tender and the mixture thickens.
4. Stir in the raisins (if using) and cook for an additional 5 minutes.
5. Remove from heat and let it cool slightly before serving. Optionally, garnish with a sprinkle of cinnamon.

Avocado Toast on Gluten-Free Bread
Ingredients:

- 2 slices gluten-free bread
- 1 ripe avocado
- 1 tablespoon olive oil
- Salt and pepper to taste
- Red pepper flakes (optional)
- Fresh lemon juice (optional)

Instructions:

1. Toast the gluten-free bread until crispy.
2. While the bread is toasting, cut the avocado in half and remove the pit. Scoop the flesh into a bowl.
3. Mash the avocado with a fork and stir in the olive oil, salt, and pepper.
4. Spread the mashed avocado mixture onto the toasted bread.
5. Optionally, sprinkle with red pepper flakes and a squeeze of fresh lemon juice. Serve immediately.

Chickpea and Spinach Stew
Ingredients:

- 1 can (15 oz) chickpeas, drained and rinsed
- 4 cups fresh spinach, chopped
- 1 tablespoon olive oil
- 1 onion, chopped
- 2 garlic cloves, minced
- 1 teaspoon cumin
- 1 teaspoon turmeric
- 1/2 teaspoon paprika
- 1 can (14.5 oz) diced tomatoes
- 1 cup vegetable broth
- Salt and pepper to taste

Instructions:

1. Heat olive oil in a large pot over medium heat.
2. Add the onion and garlic and cook for 5 minutes until softened.
3. Stir in the cumin, turmeric, and paprika, and cook for another minute until fragrant.
4. Add the chickpeas, diced tomatoes, vegetable broth, and salt and pepper to taste.
5. Bring to a boil, then reduce the heat to low and simmer for 20 minutes.
6. Stir in the spinach and cook until wilted.
7. Adjust seasoning as needed, and serve warm.

Gluten-Free Pizza with Toppings
Ingredients for the crust:

- 2 cups gluten-free flour blend
- 1 teaspoon baking powder
- 1 teaspoon salt
- 1/2 teaspoon garlic powder
- 1 tablespoon olive oil
- 3/4 cup warm water
- 1 teaspoon active dry yeast
- 1 tablespoon honey

Toppings (suggested):

- Tomato sauce
- Fresh mozzarella cheese
- Sliced mushrooms
- Pepperoni or vegetables of choice
- Fresh basil

Instructions:

1. Preheat the oven to 475°F (245°C).
2. In a small bowl, combine the warm water, yeast, and honey. Let sit for 5-10 minutes, or until foamy.
3. In a larger bowl, mix the gluten-free flour, baking powder, salt, and garlic powder.
4. Add the yeast mixture and olive oil to the dry ingredients and stir until a dough forms.
5. Roll the dough out on a piece of parchment paper into your desired shape.
6. Transfer to a baking sheet and bake for 10-12 minutes until golden brown.
7. Remove from the oven and add your desired pizza toppings.
8. Bake for an additional 5-7 minutes or until the cheese is melted and bubbly.

Pecan-Crusted Salmon

Ingredients:

- 4 salmon fillets
- 1/2 cup chopped pecans
- 1/4 cup almond flour
- 1 tablespoon Dijon mustard
- 1 tablespoon maple syrup
- 1 tablespoon olive oil
- Salt and pepper to taste

Instructions:

1. Preheat the oven to 375°F (190°C).
2. In a small bowl, combine the pecans, almond flour, salt, and pepper.
3. In a separate bowl, whisk together the Dijon mustard, maple syrup, and olive oil.
4. Brush the salmon fillets with the mustard mixture and then press them into the pecan mixture, coating both sides.
5. Place the salmon on a baking sheet lined with parchment paper.
6. Bake for 12-15 minutes, or until the salmon is cooked through and flakes easily with a fork.

Spicy Roasted Chickpeas
Ingredients:

- 1 can (15 oz) chickpeas, drained and rinsed
- 1 tablespoon olive oil
- 1 teaspoon chili powder
- 1/2 teaspoon paprika
- 1/4 teaspoon cayenne pepper
- Salt to taste

Instructions:

1. Preheat the oven to 400°F (200°C).
2. Pat the chickpeas dry with a paper towel to remove excess moisture.
3. Toss the chickpeas with olive oil, chili powder, paprika, cayenne pepper, and salt.
4. Spread the chickpeas on a baking sheet in a single layer.
5. Roast for 25-30 minutes, stirring halfway through, until crispy.
6. Let them cool slightly before serving as a snack.

Flourless Almond Cake

Ingredients:

- 2 cups almond flour
- 1/2 cup maple syrup or honey
- 4 eggs
- 1 teaspoon vanilla extract
- 1/4 cup coconut oil, melted
- 1/2 teaspoon baking powder
- 1/4 teaspoon salt

Instructions:

1. Preheat the oven to 350°F (175°C).
2. Grease a 9-inch round cake pan with coconut oil or line with parchment paper.
3. In a large bowl, whisk together the almond flour, maple syrup, eggs, vanilla extract, melted coconut oil, baking powder, and salt.
4. Pour the batter into the prepared cake pan.
5. Bake for 20-25 minutes, or until a toothpick comes out clean.
6. Let the cake cool before removing from the pan. Optionally, serve with fresh fruit or whipped cream.

Grilled Veggie Kebabs
Ingredients:

- 1 red bell pepper, cut into chunks
- 1 zucchini, sliced
- 1 red onion, cut into wedges
- 1 cup cherry tomatoes
- 8 oz mushrooms, whole or halved
- 2 tablespoons olive oil
- 1 tablespoon balsamic vinegar
- 1 teaspoon dried oregano
- Salt and pepper to taste
- Wooden skewers (soaked in water for 30 minutes)

Instructions:

1. Preheat the grill to medium-high heat.
2. In a bowl, mix the olive oil, balsamic vinegar, oregano, salt, and pepper.
3. Thread the vegetables onto the soaked wooden skewers.
4. Brush the vegetables with the olive oil mixture.
5. Grill the skewers for 8-10 minutes, turning occasionally, until the vegetables are tender and lightly charred.
6. Serve warm.

Gluten-Free Frittata
Ingredients:

- 6 large eggs
- 1/4 cup milk (dairy or non-dairy)
- 1/2 cup spinach, chopped
- 1/4 cup onion, diced
- 1/2 cup bell pepper, diced
- 1/4 cup cheese (optional, dairy-free if needed)
- 1 tablespoon olive oil
- Salt and pepper to taste

Instructions:

1. Preheat the oven to 375°F (190°C).
2. Heat the olive oil in an oven-safe skillet over medium heat.
3. Add the onion and bell pepper, cooking until softened, about 5 minutes.
4. Add the spinach and cook for another 2 minutes until wilted.
5. In a bowl, whisk together the eggs, milk, salt, and pepper. Pour the egg mixture into the skillet.
6. Cook on the stove for 3-4 minutes until the edges set.
7. Transfer the skillet to the oven and bake for 10-12 minutes, until the frittata is fully set and golden.
8. Remove from the oven, let cool for a few minutes, and slice.

Roasted Red Pepper Soup

Ingredients:

- 4 red bell peppers, roasted and peeled
- 1 onion, chopped
- 2 garlic cloves, minced
- 1 cup vegetable broth
- 1 teaspoon olive oil
- 1/2 teaspoon smoked paprika
- Salt and pepper to taste
- 1 tablespoon fresh basil (optional)

Instructions:

1. Preheat the oven to 400°F (200°C).
2. Place the bell peppers on a baking sheet and roast for 20-25 minutes until the skin blisters.
3. Peel and remove seeds from the peppers.
4. In a pot, heat olive oil over medium heat. Add the onion and garlic, cooking for 5 minutes until softened.
5. Add the roasted peppers, vegetable broth, paprika, salt, and pepper to the pot.
6. Bring to a boil, then reduce the heat and simmer for 10 minutes.
7. Use an immersion blender to blend until smooth, or transfer to a blender.
8. Serve warm, garnished with fresh basil if desired.

Gluten-Free Chocolate Mousse
Ingredients:

- 1 cup heavy cream or coconut cream
- 1/2 cup dark chocolate chips (gluten-free)
- 1 tablespoon maple syrup or sweetener of choice
- 1/2 teaspoon vanilla extract

Instructions:

1. In a small saucepan, melt the chocolate chips over low heat, stirring until smooth.
2. In a separate bowl, whip the cream until stiff peaks form.
3. Gently fold the melted chocolate into the whipped cream, adding the maple syrup and vanilla.
4. Spoon the mousse into serving dishes and chill in the fridge for at least 1 hour before serving.
5. Garnish with chocolate shavings or berries.

Quinoa and Vegetable Stir-Fry
Ingredients:

- 1 cup cooked quinoa
- 1 tablespoon olive oil
- 1 onion, sliced
- 1 carrot, julienned
- 1 zucchini, diced
- 1 cup broccoli florets
- 1/2 cup peas
- 2 tablespoons soy sauce (gluten-free)
- 1 teaspoon sesame oil
- 1/2 teaspoon ginger, grated
- Salt and pepper to taste

Instructions:

1. Heat olive oil in a large pan or wok over medium heat.
2. Add the onion and carrot, stir-frying for 2-3 minutes.
3. Add the zucchini, broccoli, and peas, cooking for an additional 5 minutes.
4. Stir in the cooked quinoa, soy sauce, sesame oil, and ginger.
5. Cook for another 3-4 minutes until heated through.
6. Season with salt and pepper, and serve.

Baked Falafel
Ingredients:

- 1 can (15 oz) chickpeas, drained and rinsed
- 1/2 cup fresh parsley
- 1/2 cup onion, chopped
- 3 cloves garlic
- 1 teaspoon cumin
- 1/2 teaspoon coriander
- 1/4 teaspoon cayenne pepper
- 1 tablespoon olive oil
- Salt and pepper to taste
- 1/4 cup gluten-free flour

Instructions:

1. Preheat the oven to 375°F (190°C).
2. In a food processor, combine chickpeas, parsley, onion, garlic, cumin, coriander, cayenne, olive oil, salt, and pepper.
3. Pulse until a coarse mixture forms.
4. Add gluten-free flour and pulse again to combine.
5. Shape the mixture into small balls or patties and place on a baking sheet lined with parchment paper.
6. Bake for 25-30 minutes, flipping halfway through, until golden brown.
7. Serve with tahini or yogurt sauce.

Gluten-Free Carrot Cake

Ingredients:

- 2 cups almond flour
- 1/2 cup coconut flour
- 1 1/2 teaspoons baking powder
- 1/2 teaspoon cinnamon
- 1/4 teaspoon nutmeg
- 1/4 teaspoon salt
- 4 large eggs
- 1/2 cup maple syrup
- 1/4 cup olive oil
- 2 cups grated carrots
- 1/2 cup chopped walnuts (optional)

Instructions:

1. Preheat the oven to 350°F (175°C).
2. In a bowl, mix the almond flour, coconut flour, baking powder, cinnamon, nutmeg, and salt.
3. In a separate bowl, whisk the eggs, maple syrup, and olive oil.
4. Stir the wet ingredients into the dry ingredients, then fold in the grated carrots and walnuts.
5. Pour the batter into a greased 9-inch cake pan.
6. Bake for 30-35 minutes or until a toothpick comes out clean.
7. Let cool before frosting (if desired).

Coconut Macaroons
Ingredients:

- 2 1/2 cups unsweetened shredded coconut
- 1/4 cup honey or maple syrup
- 2 large egg whites
- 1 teaspoon vanilla extract
- Pinch of salt

Instructions:

1. Preheat the oven to 325°F (165°C).
2. In a large bowl, mix the shredded coconut, egg whites, honey, vanilla, and salt.
3. Drop spoonfuls of the mixture onto a parchment-lined baking sheet.
4. Bake for 18-20 minutes, or until the edges are golden brown.
5. Let cool on the baking sheet before serving.

www.ingramcontent.com/pod-product-compliance
Lightning Source LLC
LaVergne TN
LVHW081338060526
838201LV00055B/2716